Wisdom Keys
for
Life

Tanya R. Taylor

Preface

Wisdom Keys for Life is a handy guide of more than one hundred thought-provoking nuggets to give you daily inspiration and help you through life's most difficult moments.

For years, I've sent out wisdom keys to practically everyone on my email list. It's just something I was compelled to do and have tried to keep up with ever since — especially now that I realize how much it means to people. Occasionally, someone would send a note stating how that particular word received was what they really needed at the moment, so I feel like the effort to get them out there is truly worth it. As quickly as these nuggets come to my mind (and they do right out of the blue), I have to jot them down so that I can pass them on.

A Scottish friend of mine, Fay Knowles, who writes romance novels was quite intrigued by the wisdom keys. She suggested that I compile them into book form so that people can have them readily available whenever they need an encouraging word. So, here they are and thanks very much, Fay, for the wise suggestion!

I hope that you, the reader, finds them as encouraging and uplifting as I do myself.

All the best.

1 Your greatest lessons often come as a result of your greatest pain. In that pain, could lie your greatest treasure. Use what you've learned to improve yourself and to positively impact those around you. Never waste your pain.

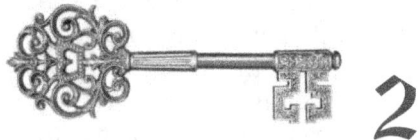

2

A day spent worrying is a day totally wasted. Consider this: Has worrying ever solved a single problem for you?

3

Every moment you spend reflecting on the pain and disappointments of your past is a moment you have stolen from your life.

4

No matter how many times *lied upon*, *kicked down*, *slandered* or *betrayed*, if a person is determined to succeed—though in pain—he will ignore the lies, keep getting back up, ignore his haters, slanderers and betrayers, and carry his unseen torch straight on to victory.

5 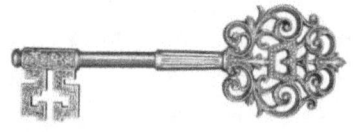 Instead of focusing on all the things that are wrong with your life, why not focus on what's right? If you focus on the things that matter the most that have absolutely nothing to do with material things, you can get through the toughest of times with a strength and endurance you never knew you had.

 **6**

Your perception of a matter directly affects your feelings. By deciding (ahead of time such as at the start of the day) that you are going to remain in peace, will successfully override and dampen the power of any negativity that may come your way.

7

The light is definitely at the end of the tunnel. You just have to be strong and patient enough to get there. If you refuse to give up, you will most certainly arrive.

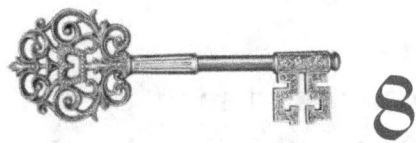

8

When you are grateful for everything, you have very little to no time to complain about anything.

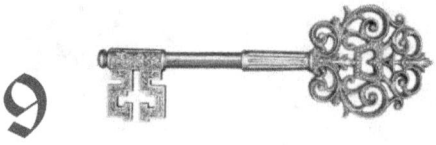

9

If you cannot envision it, there's a good chance you will never have it.

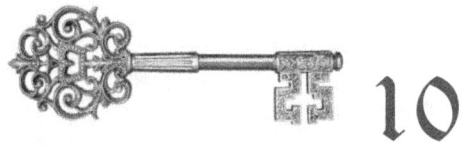

10

Don't be overly concerned about other people's attitude toward you. Be more concerned about keeping your attitude in check and your peace in tact in spite of their cruelty.

11

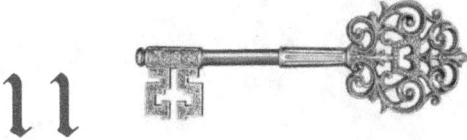

The "high road" is never a road low-minded people take. Don't let these people offend you lest you descend to their level of mediocre thinking. Think: "High road equals success, favor, open doors & limitless opportunities. Low road equals: Obstacles, hindrances, blockages, mishaps & regret."

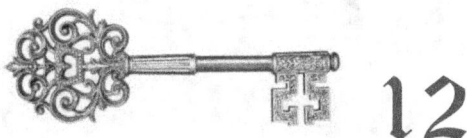

12

Things might be really bad, but they could always be worse. That alone should give you some consolation.

13

If you crumble into little bits and pieces when the world turns against you, you would have given them exactly what they wanted. Stand tall when all fingers are cruelly pointing in your direction. Eventually, those behind them will get tired and walk away.

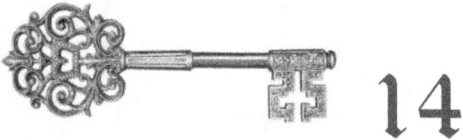 14

Don't look for the easy way of doing things. Look for the *right* way. Your effort of looking for *right*, instead of *easy* will cause you to reap wonderful rewards down the line.

15

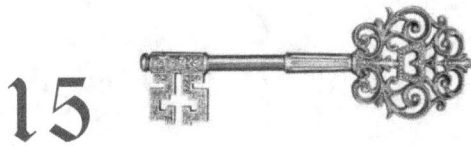

When you finally come to the realization that it's not all about you, then you're on your way to making serious progress.

16

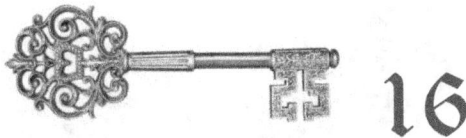

Always sow good seeds of compassion, love and kindness to reap a good harvest in life. It's not a matter of *if* the harvest will come, it is only a matter of *when.*

17

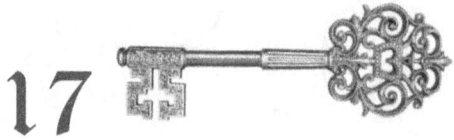

No problem that has presented itself should leave without us learning something that will enhance the quality of our lives. A life-altering lesson (no matter how small) is hidden in every problem.

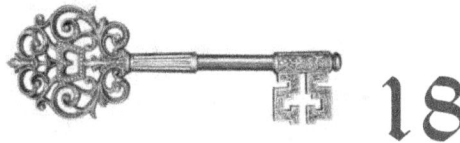

18

Never take another person for granted. If you could see the treasure God placed inside of that individual that he, himself, might not even realize, you will be totally astounded.

19

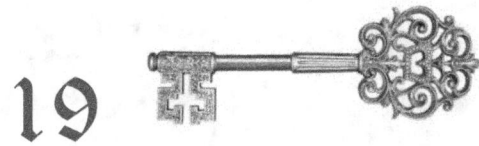

God's Divine Favor is what you need in your life. It can do for you what money cannot buy. However, the heart must be pure and your motives right.

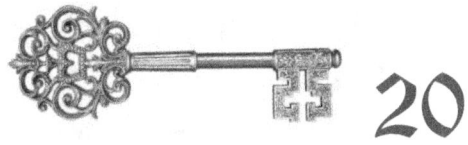

20

If you thought for a moment that your intellect, education or charisma got you to the level you're proud to be at, you have been so sadly deceived. Without God, you would have no intellect, education or charisma. Without Him - you have nothing, are nothing and can do nothing. He creates the pathway, opens all the doors, and He alone deserves All the praise.

21

The less complaining you do, the further
you'll make it up the hill.

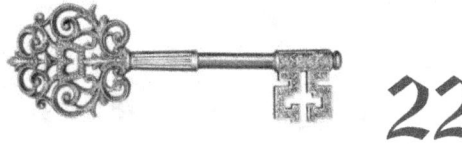

22

No one is going to truly respect you until
you understand what it means to respect
yourself.

23

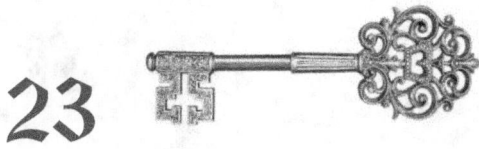

Difficulty is never a hindrance, but is used by the wise as a <u>Motivator.</u>

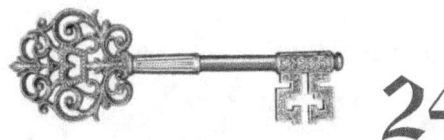

24

Throwing yourself a pity party makes you more pitiful than you thought you were before.

25

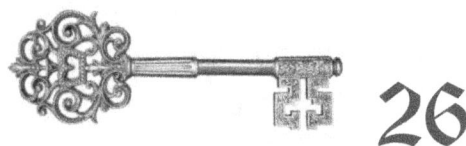

Before you ask for someone's advice, make sure that you are not *only* willing to accept it if it happens to be what you want to hear. If you are not willing to accept sound advice regardless of how difficult the truth may be, do not waste the other person's time. Instead, if stubbornness prevails, continue the pretense that you know all things and have it all-together while your life gradually falls apart.

26

Once you don't give up—as difficult as it may be—you can overcome.

27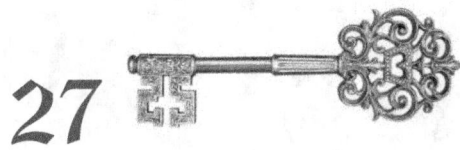

Your biggest hindrance to success is oftentimes your own negative thoughts.

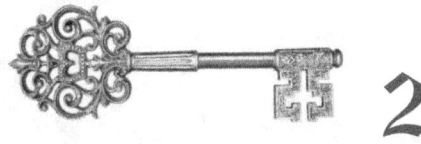 ## 28

Not every day will be the same, but your attitude should remain the same - providing that you have a good one.

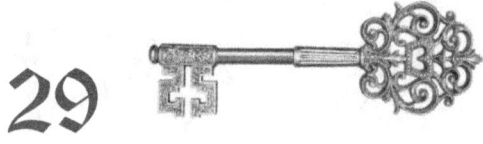

29

Allowing Jealousy into your heart is like cancer in your bones. Learning to be happy for others is pure rejuvenation and restoration to the body and soul.

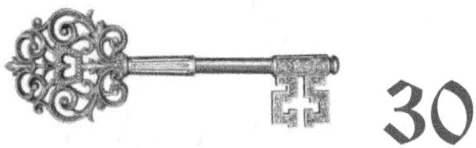

30

No matter how hard you try, you can <u>never</u> talk sense into the head of a fool.

31

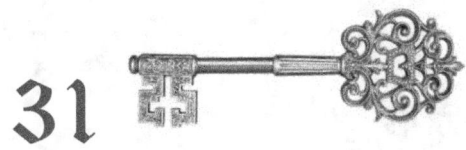

Each day presents its own problems. The fact is that <u>no one</u> has the power to *steal* your peace. In order to lose it, you would have to willingly *give it away.* When you are truly connected to God (which goes way beyond going to church and singing hymns), *no* human being, *no* situation can rob you of your peace.

32 Even when

no one believes in you, *<u>believe in yourself.</u>* Use their rejection as fuel for progress and success.

33

Being here on earth in our human bodies, we sometimes forget that we are actually spirit beings. The real 'us' lives inside the earthly suit. Spiritual connections are far more powerful than anything that has to do with this earthly realm.

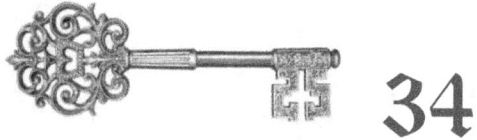

34

Self-absorption sucks out your joy, contentment, peace and gratitude — keeps you from deliverance, victory and wisdom. Self-absorption works against you in more ways than one.

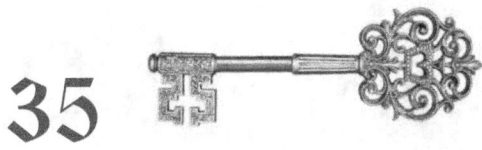

35

Every day of our lives we are planting seeds - whether good or bad - from which we will reap a harvest. If we are wise, we will do our endeavor best to plant the good ones.

36

It takes true humility to apologize for an offense without defending your actions in the process. Sincere apologies must be void of excuses however logical they may seem.

37

Some people will continuously disrespect you and insult your intelligence as long as you allow them to think that it's perfectly okay. Pay close attention to *actions*—they tell you all you need to know.

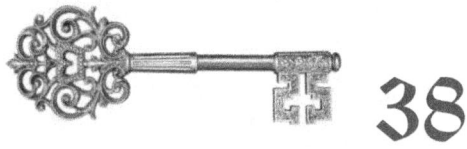

38

When your heart aches for others who are suffering even though you, yourself are suffering, then you know that your heart is a sweet sight in the Eyes of God. His blessings & favor will rest upon you and will never leave you.

39

Having a Spirit of Excellence means you do what is right and to the best of your ability — not for human accolades — but because God is watching.

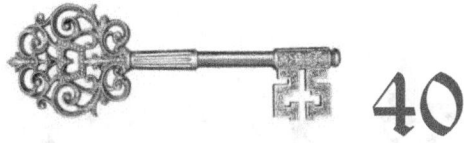 40

Your perception of a matter makes all the difference in the world. If you can envision the light at the end of the tunnel, with steady, forward movement, eventually - you will get there.

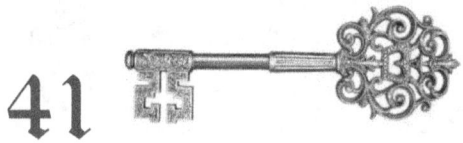

41

Your greatest roadblock should propel you towards your greatest fight. Undaunting persistence is the key to victory.

42 You cannot make it to the other side if you are not willing to climb the mountain. Those who succeed in life are the ones who kept climbing even as the circumstances became unbearably difficult. Persistence brings freedom.

43

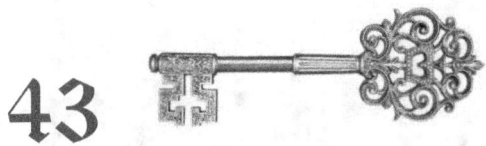

You cannot get ahead if you continue to look behind. Living in the past is a sure way to remain stagnated.

44

You have not finished the final chapter of your life until the last word is written. Until then, keep pressing on and moving forward to fulfill your life's purpose. Don't give up: There's still more to do.

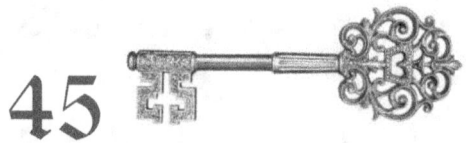

45 If you allow yourself to be controlled by the opinion of others - where what they think (mere human beings) matters more to you than what God thinks - then you would have made them your god. And while you have done that, you would have dishonored the One who created you.

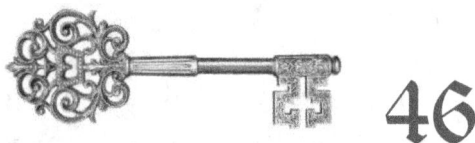

46

When you are in love with God and people desperately want to see you fail, the higher and faster He will elevate you — and the more He smiles at His handiwork.

47 The way to *feel* good is to *do* good. When you do nice gestures and care for others daily - even the ones you don't know, you are rewarding yourself with the best feeling in the world that has its roots in Love. Otherwise, misery is your company.

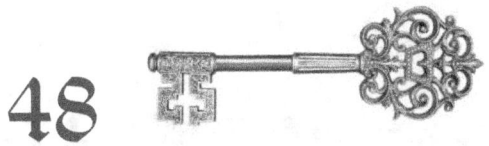

48

When it comes to friendship, know that *quantity* is not what matters. It's no use having many friends and none of them are there for you through thick and thin or truly loves you. Look for *quality*: Commitment, loyalty, acceptance, love. This is what matters and this is what causes friendships to last a lifetime.

49   Be mindful to have the right folks in your corner. When the wrong ones are there, whether you know it or not, you are on a downward spiral. Good people uplift you. Subtle haters drag you down every chance they get.

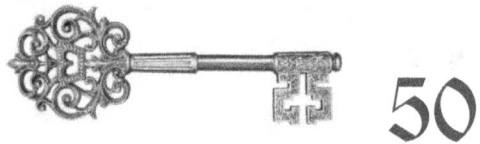 **50**

Being a slave to a fellow human being, many times, starts with giving his opinion more weight than you should.

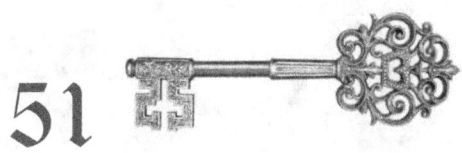

51

It's not what others think of you that really matters. Ultimately, it's what you think of yourself. The danger with that is when you don't have a healthy personal perspective (whether you think too lowly or too highly of yourself). If you see yourself the way God sees you, you will ultimately be all that He created you to be.

52

Don't give up on your dreams and aspirations in spite of the rocky path. If you are persistent enough to succeed even if you have to crawl to get there, eventually, you *will* get there.

53

Regardless of what they really are or their reason for being, it is always best to view problems as an opportunity for growth and to find the lessons in them to be learned—however painful those situations may be.

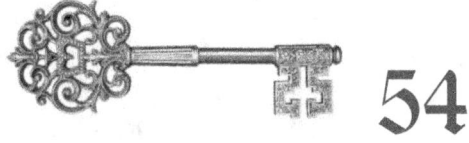

54

What you do today plays a huge role in where you end up tomorrow.

55

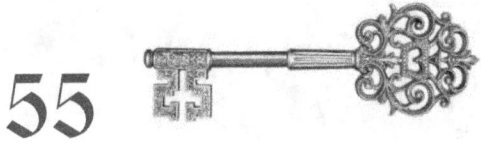

The one that judges the harshest is usually more sinful/guilty than the accused, as the spirit of pride has long set up habitation within his very soul, oftentimes, without him even recognizing it.

56

No one can 'put a value' on you based on what you have or don't have. They were not the One who created you and you are incapable of being appraised. Everyone was created in God's image and is therefore 'unappraisable' (too valuable beyond estimation).

57

Greatness comes with great responsibilities, but also with great difficulties. No one considered 'great' had a challenge-free or struggle-free life. The challenges and struggles, heart-aches and betrayals were all necessary on the road to that exceptional existence.

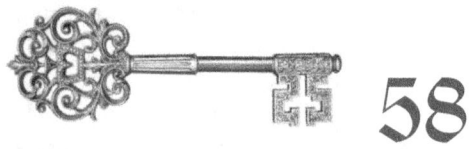

58

Your greatest reward is not in your sacrifice - it's in your obedience.

59   When you love God *totally* and *unconditionally*, you'll submit your will to <u>His will</u> trusting Him wholeheartedly, with unshakeable confidence that He has the very best in mind for you.

60   If anyone views himself as being totally perfect in the actual sense of the word, he is undoubtedly *imperfect* in God's eyes. For the thought alone is one of presumption, impurity and imperfection. One may rightly strive for perfection pertaining to character and spirit, but must bear in mind that he will never reach its purest form within this human body. The fact that he has strived for it until the end has made him 'perfect' in the eyes of God.

61

What do you do when you feel like you've been beaten down in life? Get back up and keep going even if you must *crawl* to your destination.

62

Anyone with any wisdom at all is aware of his own mortality - that he does not own the breath he breathes and that not even the next moment is promised to him. If we all keep this serious thought in mind, we'd be sure to always treat each other respectfully, repent often and repent sincerely.

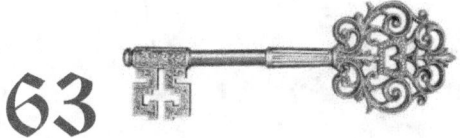

63

Take inventory — check the state of your own heart. Keep your eyes from judging others around you. They may be making the mistakes with a heart that means well, while you are making *less mistakes* with a *filthy* heart. Man focuses on the actions, while God looks at the heart.

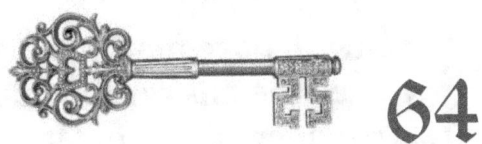

64

God will never withhold what's best from those whose <u>love</u> for Him is *unconditional* and whose <u>trust</u> in Him is *unwavering.*

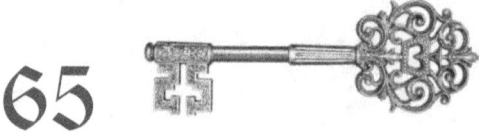

65

Your greatest struggle often precedes your greatest blessing. Unfortunately, so many have given up at the tail end of the fight.

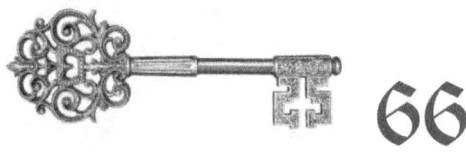

66

How to know when you have matured spiritually: When you see the answer to your prayers *through spiritual eyes*, holding fast to it against all resistance, and your faith not shaken by what you observe in the natural realm.

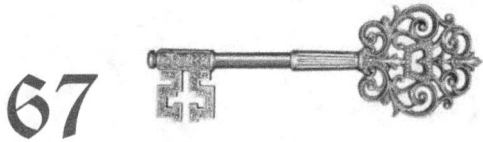

67

When you so tightly hold on to your past,
you cannot move on to your future.

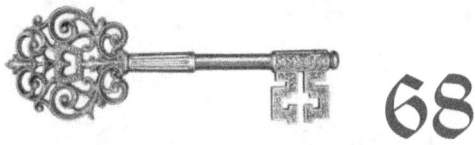

68

The fact that God instructs us to forgive does
not suggest that the malicious offense
perpetrated against us has been unnoticed or
overlooked by Him. Forgiveness frees us from
emotional and spiritual captivity that can
only pull us down. Yet, one who knows God
understands that He will correct the wrong
and no revenge thought of by the human
mind can compare with God's means of
justice. Trusting God is forgiving quickly,
forgiving completely and moving on.

69 If you decide to view your challenges more as opportunities for advancement, you will realize that eventually everything will fall neatly into place and you will be living a purposeful life. If you avoid the challenges - you shun the opportunities.

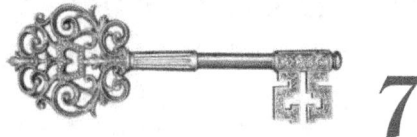

Control your thoughts and you will control your life (your feelings, your responses).

71

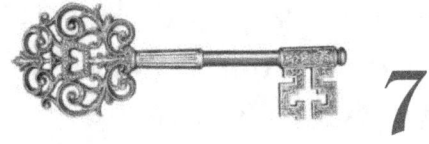

Enjoy the moments of each day; do not waste them with worry.

72

An irrefutable reality is that we will never see this day again. Within each day lies countless opportunities for each one of us to make a positive difference in some way — in our own lives and in the lives of others. When we bypass those opportunities, we bypass the blessings attached to each one of them. See each day as one loaded with great potential and never to be wasted because the fact of the matter is: When it's gone, it's gone for good. Make the most out of each day for every day is a priceless gift from God.

73

When, as adults, we've arrived at the end of our lives, we will be confronted with one major question by God: *What type of fruit did you bear?* That applies mainly to our actions. Consider this: Would anyone *outside* of your immediate family or inner circle be able to say that you were a positive influence on their life? Or would you have to face God with the knowledge that you lived only for yourself and your loved ones - that no one else He created mattered to you? What a serious thought to consider and a frightening position to be in.

74

In order to move forward, you must stop looking behind.

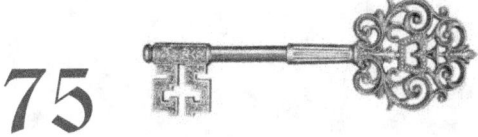

75

God has the best plan for your life. You will only walk into it if you humbly submit your will to His will - totally, without restraint.

76 If you are looking for a *perfect saint*, you will never find one. True saints are always aware of their sinful nature and they never allow themselves to forget it. That's what keeps them humble and that's what makes them holy.

77

It is very difficult to continue doing the right thing when all the wrong things are happening. Every part of your being screams to forget - to just give up as nothing seems to be working. However, take heart that with every action, there is a reaction. Every good deed is a good seed planted into the soil of your life that will reap a great harvest when you least expect it. Keep doing good; continue pressing on and never give up. You have to go *through* it in order to get *to* it.

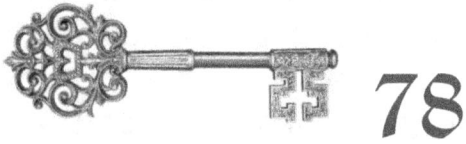

78

If you are constantly concerned about what others think, you are a slave to those around you.

79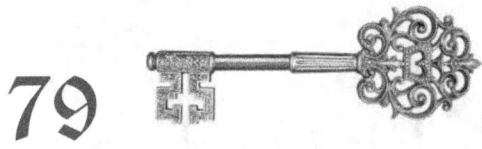

If the love you claim to have for God is real, you cannot reject Him when faced with immense difficulty and trials. Even if tempted to leave, you will surely return — for the love in your heart for Him will always draw you back.

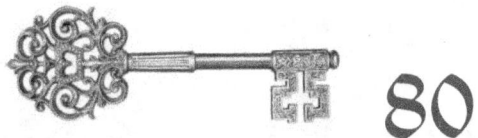 # 80

He who is wise possesses a treasure more valuable than the most precious stone.

81

When God is truly your Best Friend, you
don't have time to worry about your
enemies.

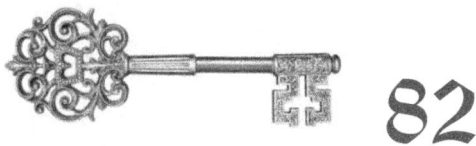

82

We are never failures when we've put forth
our greatest effort in the face of our greatest
challenges.

83

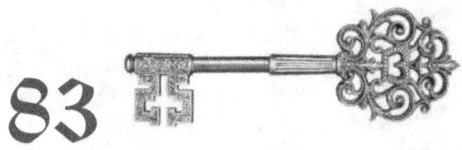

Each day presents a new opportunity for Growth. Embrace the process - instead of despising it.

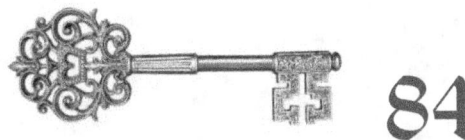

84

Do not be discouraged by failure. Instead, use it as motivation to succeed.

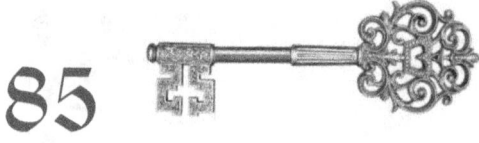

85

Your passion, if not ignored, will take you to your destiny.

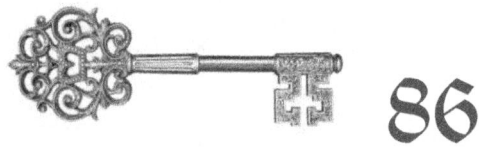

86

If God is willing to forgive you, you must be willing to forgive yourself. If He casts your sin into the sea of forgetfulness, why should you carry it with you everywhere you go?

87

God always gives us what we need when we need it. Don't despair; He is never late.

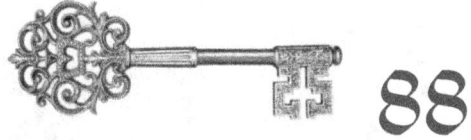

88

Love is the only answer to this world's many problems, but it must be pure from one to another—wanting the best and believing the best.

89  You may think that everyone can only see the surface, but God sees inside your heart. He who does not do daily inventory is full of pride and arrogance, and only fooling himself.

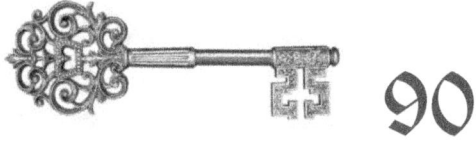 **90**

Let God's love for you guide you through your journey of life - through all the challenges and victories. Hold His hand and never let go.

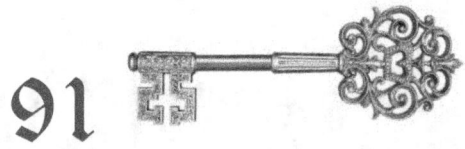

91

All we have in this world is love. With it, we have everything. Without it, we have *NOTHING*.

92
The closer you are to God, the more you see your own faults and yearn to be better. No one close to God remains in denial - refusing to acknowledge the true image of himself that he sees in the mirror.

93 When suffering through a heart-wrenching situation, if in the midst of it, you can still manage to say *"God, I love you"* and mean it, undoubtedly, you have matured spiritually and have established a real connection with the Creator of this universe–our Father. With that in mind, you can rest assured that you will get through that difficulty, rise above the pain and emerge victorious in every area of your life. Your unconditional love for God will steer you into the miraculous.

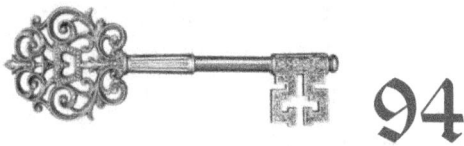

94

Even in the darkest tunnel, there's light at the end of it.

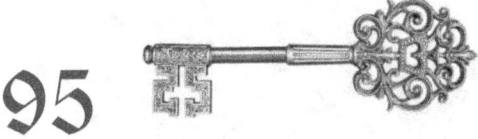

95

The moment you thought it was all about
you the devil fooled you.

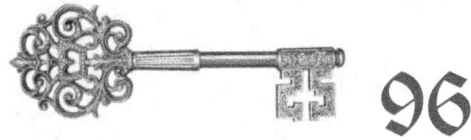

96

If someone were to ask: What is the first
thing you think about upon waking each
morning? If your immediate answer is not
"God", then without a doubt, your priorities
are not in order. Remember why you are
here to begin with. When He is the first
thought in your mind upon opening your
eyes to a new day, you are honoring Him
with a pure and infinite love. Nothing and
no one should mean more to you.

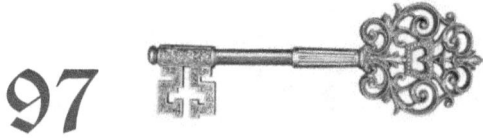

97

Those of you who truly love The Lord, don't view your disappointment as a set-back, but instead as a *set-up* for God's floodgates to open wide on your behalf.

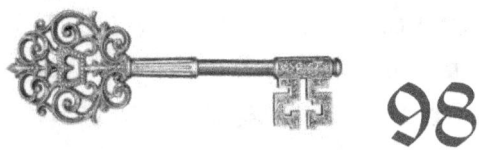

98

If you ever feel like your life is going nowhere, remember that there is no meaningless existence on the face of this planet. Your journey matters and has a purpose attached to it.

99

The absence of hope is a major cause of depression. The fact that one's circumstances appear bleak and unchangeable feeds what, in the mind, is a personal reality. However, true hope and faith glares in the face of one's dismal surroundings, painful plights and seemingly insurmountable challenges. As long as one can envision a brighter future, his hope remains alive and becomes the vehicle which will take him toward that future reality. Steady hope in the midst of trials will ultimately make the seemingly impossible - possible.

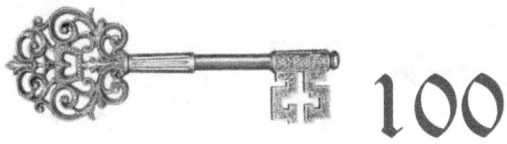

100

God will never *force* you to go where He wants to take you. You must be *willing*.

101

Every day, you have the power to positively impact someone's life. The question you must ask yourself is: *'Do I want to?'* Your ability to say 'yes' has absolutely nothing to do with your current situation. Even in dire circumstances, you can be a light that shines briskly through the darkness. The bottom line is: What you do for others, God will do for you. When you plant good seeds into the life of others, those seeds will reap a bountiful, supernatural harvest in your own life.

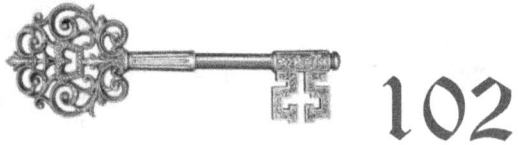

102

If you focus on your heart—on your motivation for doing things--you will know exactly where you stand with God.

Buried Dreams
(A Little Something to Think About Along Life's Journey)

You may have heard something to the effect of: "The graveyard is full of unrealized goals, unlived dreams and untapped-into potential". In other words, it simply means that many people have died having not lived their lives to their absolute, fullest potential. By the same token, I'm sure that some people tried to live their dream and worked really hard at it, but unfortunately, for some reason or the other didn't see it materialize.

Achieving great things by use of our gifts and talents oftentimes do not come easily. People who have become majorly successful in life will probably tell you that it took a lot of blood, sweat and tears, serious thoughts of wanting to give up, and episodes of utter hopelessness after seeing no way that things can possibly work out in their favor. Yet, they are now living those dreams and finally able to exhale. You may wonder what it took; how they made it and the simple answer to that is: Indomitable Persistence. *Persistence* in the face of difficulty; *persistence* in the face of opposition & ridicule; *persistence* in the face of hopelessness & despair; drying

the tears, dusting themselves off and getting back up —
and repeating that scenario over and over again.

The road to realizing your dream is not an easy one to
travel. It is a terribly rough surface filled with
unbelievably huge potholes that require a great test of
your fortitude and faith to get across. You must be able
to envision that beautiful, smoothly paved road on the
other side although it is nowhere in sight. The bottom
line is the desire to achieve your dream must be far
beyond the comprehension of others; it must be glued to
and ingrained in every fiber of your being. Otherwise,
when the road gets rough (and it will) you will throw in
the towel and put it aside – probably forever – and those
goals, dreams & aspirations will join the millions of
others in the graveyard. If it's not difficult enough to test
every bit of determination in your soul, then it's not truly
your dream, your goal, your aspiration. I believe we can
all achieve whatever level of success appointed to us;
many times we get so discouraged and give up just
before the breakthrough. If only we can see how close
we really are.

- Tanya R. Taylor -

Tanya R. Taylor is a bestselling author of both fiction and non-fiction books. Her book *CORNELIUS* was #1 in Amazon's Teen & Young-adult Multi-generational Family Fiction category.

Some Fiction Titles by This Author

Cornelius

INFESTATION: A Small Town Nightmare

Real Illusions series:

(The Awakening)
(Rebirth)
(Bone of My Bone)

Website: www.tanyaRtaylor.com